Gravity

by Grace Hansen

BEGINNING SCIENCE

Abdo Kids Jumbo is an Imprint of Abdo Kids
abdopublishing.com

abdopublishing.com

Published by Abdo Kids, a division of ABDO, P.O. Box 398166, Minneapolis, Minnesota 55439.
Copyright © 2019 by Abdo Consulting Group, Inc. International copyrights reserved in all countries.
No part of this book may be reproduced in any form without written permission from the publisher.
Abdo Kids Jumbo™ is a trademark and logo of Abdo Kids.

052018

092018

Photo Credits: Alamy, iStock, Shutterstock

Production Contributors: Teddy Borth, Jennie Forsberg, Grace Hansen

Design Contributors: Dorothy Toth, Laura Mitchell

Library of Congress Control Number: 2017960569

Publisher's Cataloging-in-Publication Data

Names: Hansen, Grace, author.

Title: Gravity / by Grace Hansen.

Description: Minneapolis, Minnesota : Abdo Kids, 2019. | Series: Beginning science |
    Includes glossary, index and online resources (page 24).

Identifiers: ISBN 9781532108075 (lib.bdg.) | ISBN 9781532109058 (ebook) |
    ISBN 9781532109546 (Read-to-me ebook)

Subjects: LCSH: Gravity--Juvenile literature. | Gravitation--Juvenile literature.

Classification: DDC 531.14--dc23

Table of Contents

What is Gravity?

Isaac Newton discovered gravity more than 300 years ago. He watched an apple fall to the ground. He knew that a **force** had to be acting on it.

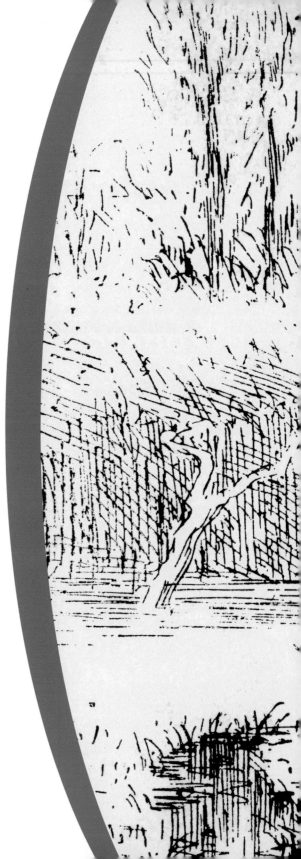

5

Gravity is a **force**. It pulls things made of **matter** toward each other.

Gravity & Matter

Everything is made of **matter**.

Humans are made of matter.

Earth is made of matter.

Things with more **matter** have a stronger **gravitational pull**. Earth is massive. Its gravitational pull is very strong. That is why everything on Earth stays there.

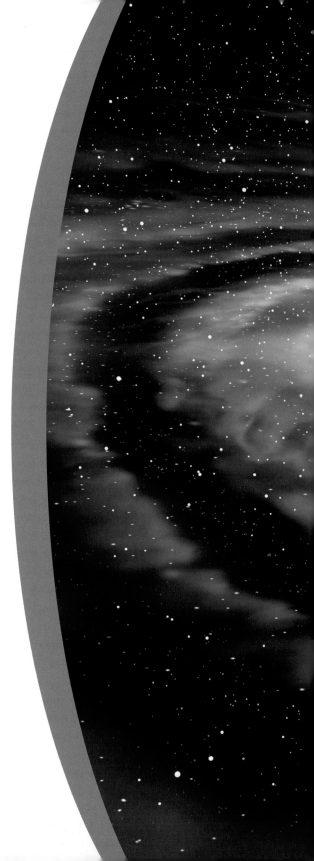

Into Space

Gravity does not just

affect things on Earth.

It keeps our galaxy in place!

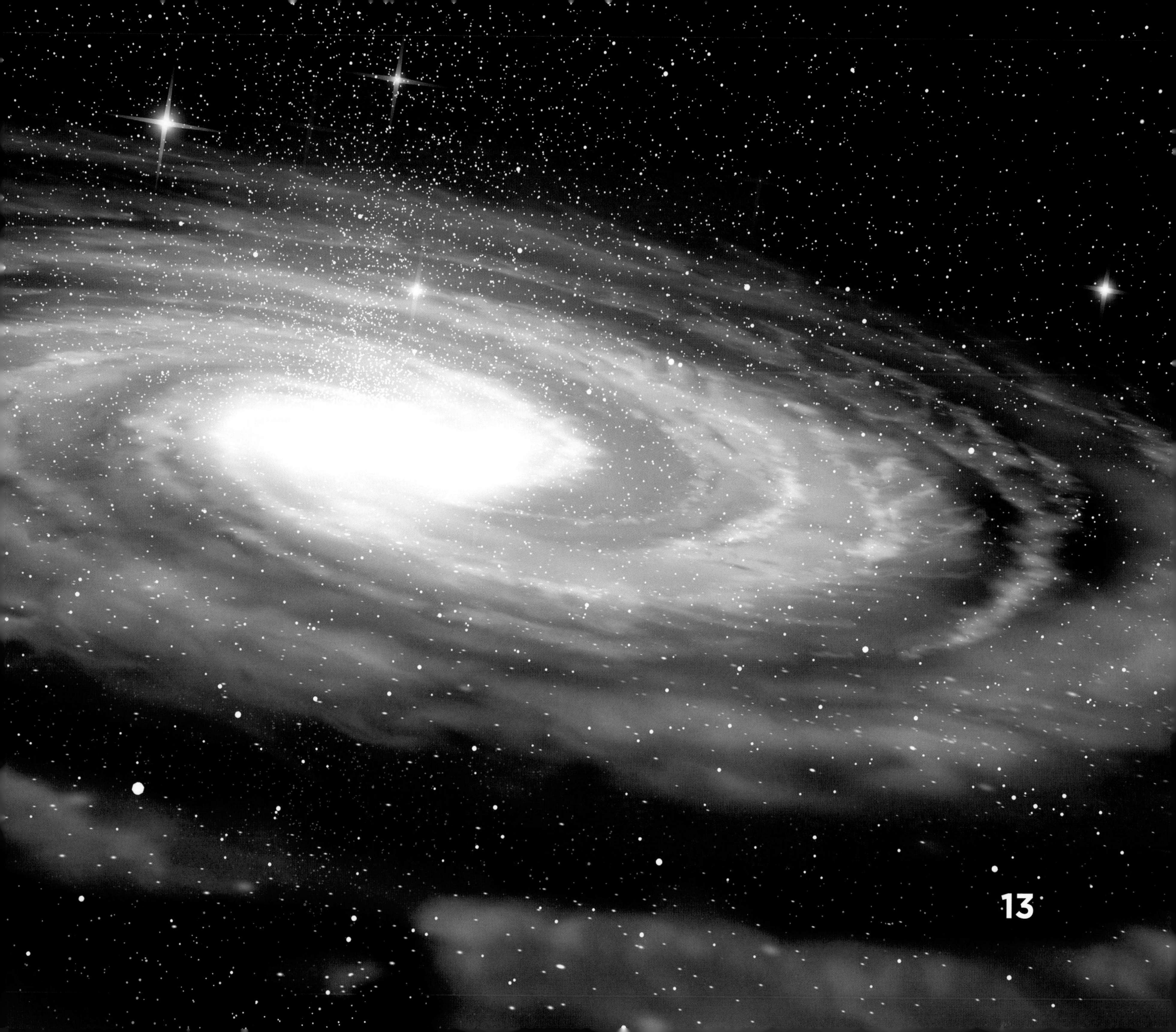

Things with a lot of **mass** want to move forward. The moon has a lot of mass and moves forward. But it is also being pulled toward Earth by Earth's gravity.

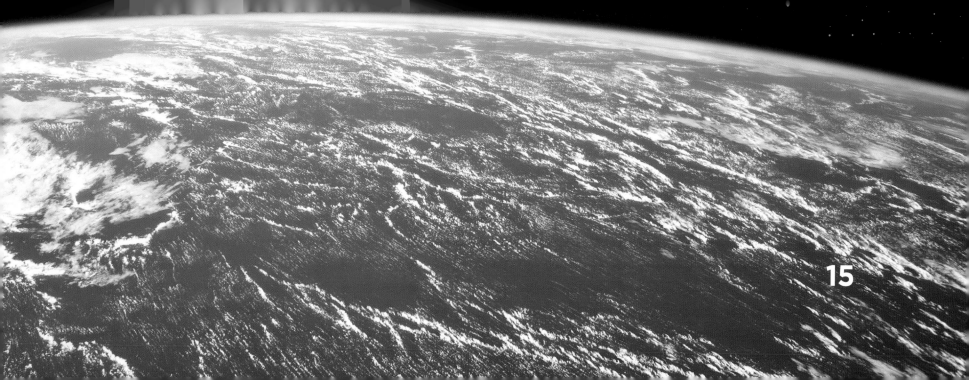

15

The moon's forward motion pulls it away from Earth. But Earth's gravity pulls it in. The **forces balance** out and the moon stays in **orbit**.

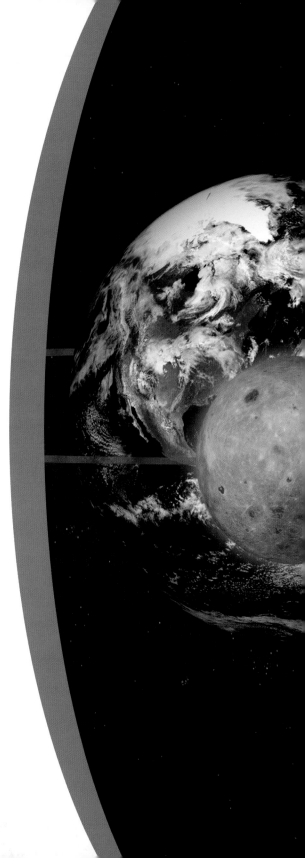

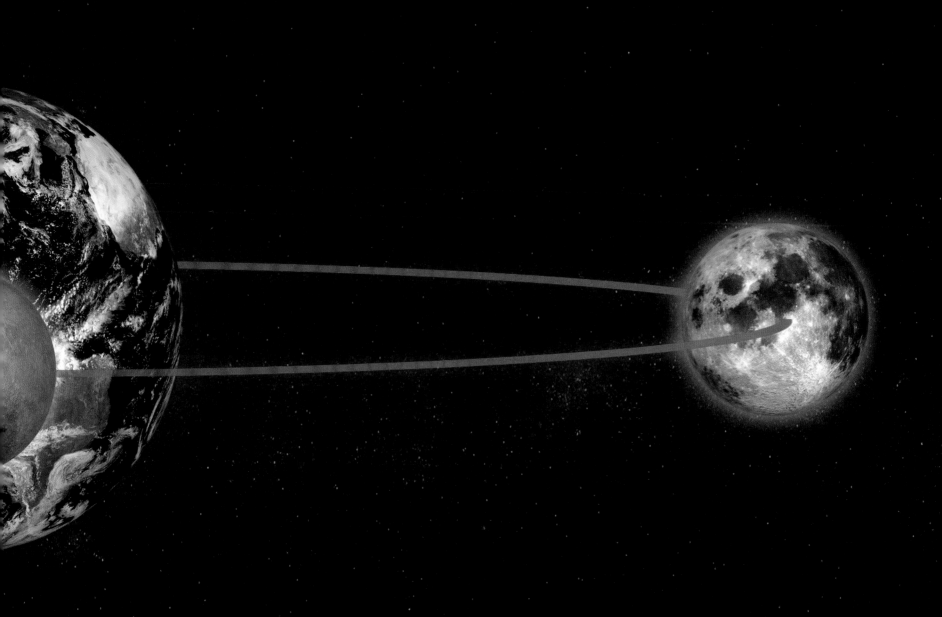

The moon **orbits** Earth. Earth and other planets orbit the Sun. Everything in space orbits the center of our galaxy. This is all due to the **force** of gravity.

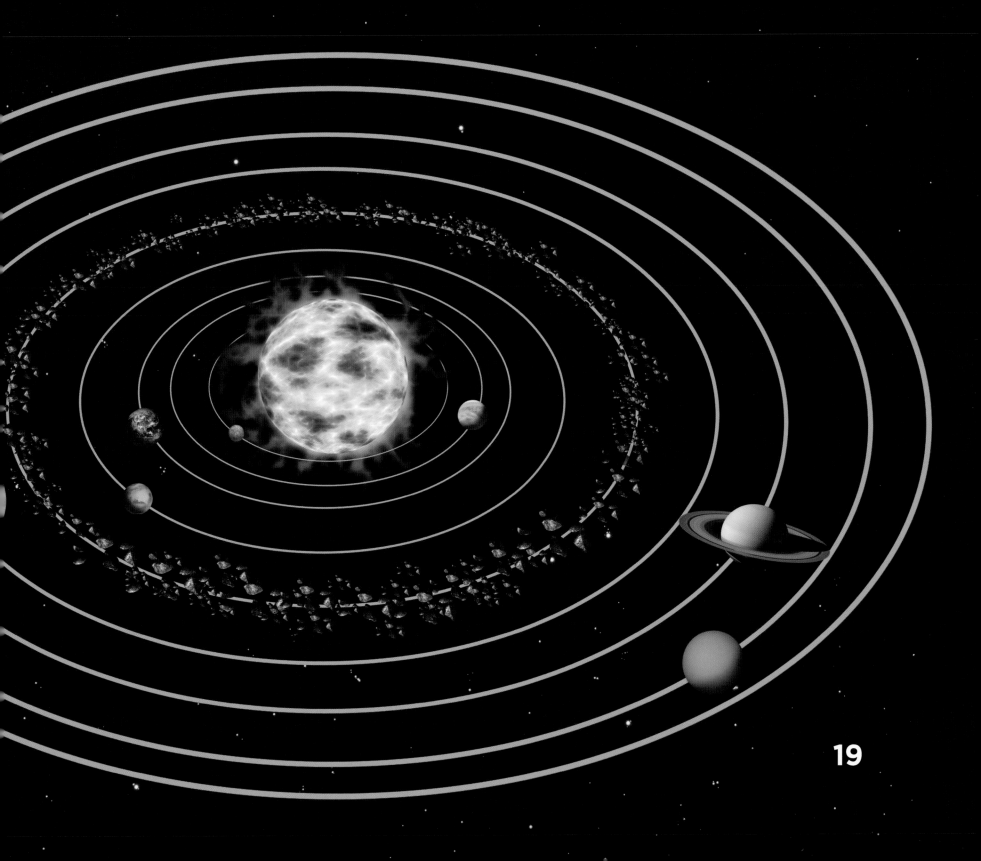

Life

Without gravity, there would not be life on Earth. You can thank gravity the next time you fall down!

Let's Review!

- Gravity is a **force** that attracts two objects that have **mass**.

- Objects with greater mass have a stronger **gravitational pull**.

- The gravitational force between two objects becomes smaller the farther apart they are.

- Gravity and forward motion keep objects in **orbit**.

Glossary

balance – the state in which opposite forces are equal.

force – a push or pull upon an object that happens when another object acts on it. With gravity, the two objects do not have to touch.

gravitational pull – attraction caused by gravity.

mass – how much matter there is in something. Mass is not the same as weight.

matter – all things that contain atoms and take up space.

orbit – a curved path in which a planet or other space body moves in a circle around another body.

Index

Abdo Kids
ONLINE
FREE! ONLINE MULTIMEDIA RESOURCES

Visit **abdokids.com** and use this code to access crafts, games, videos, and more!

Abdo Kids Code:
BGK8075